RUN WITH ME, NIKE!

Written by Cassandra Case
Illustrated by Dan Brown

Soundprints
Where Children Discover...

For Jessa—my own Nike—and for Bekki, Justin, and William—C.C.

For two wonderful parents — D.B.

Illustrations copyright © 1999 Dan Brown.
Book copyright © 1999 Futech Interactive Products, Inc., Phoenix, AZ 85018
and the Smithsonian Institution, Washington, DC 20560.

Published by Soundprints, an imprint of Futech Interactive Products, Inc., 353 Main Avenue,
Norwalk, Connecticut 06851.

Book Layout: Scott Findlay
Editor: Judy Gitenstein

First Edition 1999
10 9 8 7 6 5 4 3 2 1
Printed in Hong Kong

Acknowledgments:
    Our thanks to Jane Walsh and Dr. Gus Van Beek of the Department of Anthropology at the
Smithsonian Institution's National Museum of Natural History for their curatorial review.

Library of Congress Cataloging-in-Publication Data

Case, Cassandra
    Run with me, Nike: the Olympics in 420 B.C. / written by Cassandra Case; illustrated by Dan
Brown. — 1st ed.
        p.   cm. — (Odyssey)
    Summary: While visiting the Origins of Western Culture exhibit at the Smithsonian's Museum of
Natural History, Tomas finds himself back in time, competing in the Olympic Games in ancient Greece.
    ISBN 1-56899-604-7 (hardcover) ISBN 1-56899-605-5 (pbk.)
    [1. Olympics—Fiction. 2. Greece—Fiction. 3. Time travel—Fiction.] I. Brown, Dan, ill.
    II. Title.   III. Series: Odyssey (Smithsonian Institution)
I. Brown, Dan, ill. II. Title. III. Series: Odyssey (Smithsonian Institution)
PZ7.C2669Ru 1999   99-19244
[E]—dc21   CIP
                                                                            AC

RUN WITH ME, NIKE!

ODYSSEY

SMITHSONIAN INSTITUTION

Tomas, Lucy, Emma, and Kevin are visiting the Origins of Western Culture exhibit at the Smithsonian Institution's National Museum of Natural History. Tomas rushes ahead, taking the stairs two at a time.

"I'm in training," he calls over his shoulder.

"For what? The Olympics?" jokes Kevin.

"Maybe one day," Tomas answers. "But for now I just hope to make the track team."

In the section on ancient Greece, the four friends look at the model of the Acropolis, the hill in Athens where the Parthenon was built. Emma starts to sketch and Lucy gets out her camera.

"Look at all the pathways and steps down the side of the Acropolis!" Tomas says.

"*Those* stairs would *really* get you in shape, Tomas!" jokes Lucy, and everyone laughs.

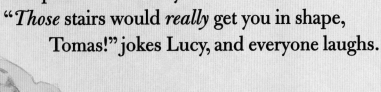

Tomas measures himself against the life-size figures in the mural painted on the wall beside the exhibit. "I'm almost as tall as a man was in ancient Greece!" he says.

"Come look at these silver coins!" says Kevin. He bends over a display case to get a closer look.

But Tomas is looking at a painted image of two men running a race. He is drawn to it because the runners look strong and eager.

"Faster, faster!" a voice calls from a distance.

Tomas is running barefoot over grass. He can hear others running behind him. They are all racing toward a group of men wearing white tunics.

Tomas can see that another boy is about to pass him. Tomas puts on a burst of speed and manages to get alongside the boy as they cross the line at the end of the field.

One of the men pats Tomas on the shoulder. "I knew you had it in you, Timon," the man says. "Now walk around a bit to cool yourself down."

Tomas can only nod. He is too out of breath to speak.

"I think your nephew has had enough training for today, Demetrios," another man calls. "He needs to save strength for the Olympiad."

The Olympiad? Tomas thinks. *I'm in ancient Greece! This man is my trainer for the Olympics!*

Tomas follows the other runners into a low, stone building. They rinse off in a shallow pool. Then they lower themselves into a large well of very hot water. Tomas is glad they don't stay in very long.

When they are done with the baths, the boys run to a courtyard and dive into a huge swimming pool. The cool spring water circulates through spouts and fountains.

After their swim, the boys dry off in rough linen sheets. The trainers rub oil on their skin, then scrape off the oil with curved, dull blades.

"Here is your chiton, Timon," calls a boy named Milo as he tosses Tomas a ball of cloth. Tomas sees that it is a short linen tunic.

"Well, Demetrios, Athens has a fine candidate for the games!" says one of the trainers.

"Thank you," says Demetrios. He smiles at Tomas. "Our patron chooses wisely. We are lucky to have of one of the most powerful citizens of Athens for our sponsor."

As everyone is leaving the baths, a young man runs up.

"Uncle Demetrios!" he calls. "The charioteer broke his arm and can't drive!"

The boy then sees Tomas and grabs his shoulders with excitement. "Brother, guess what?" he says. "Our patron asked *me* to be his charioteer in the Olympiad!"

"That is good news!" exclaims Tomas happily.

"It is a great honor, Luko!" says Demetrios, clapping the boy on the back. Everyone congratulates Luko as they walk into Olympia. The city is filled with activity. They pass food stalls, men reciting poetry, jugglers, and vendors selling doves, rabbits, pigs, and goats.

A procession passes by, leading a white bull covered with garlands. The group follows, and they come to a street lined with temples.

13

"Now is a good time to ask the gods for favor in the games," Demetrios tells the boys.

"Come on, Timon." Milo tugs Tomas's arm. "Let's go to the biggest temple and see the statue of the god Zeus. My father says it is the most wondrous statue in the world. The city-state of Elis even stamps it on their coins. Look!" Milo holds out a coin showing Zeus on a throne.

The boys enter the temple, then stop short. The statue is forty feet high! They look up in awe at Zeus's huge body, made of smooth ivory and draped in a robe of shimmering, carved gold. Zeus is sitting on an enormous gold throne of ebony wood that is inlaid with jewels.

Standing in the palm of Zeus's right hand is a smaller statue of a winged woman. She seems tiny compared to Zeus.

"It is good to be in Zeus's favor," Demetrios says as he enters the temple. "I notice that you are also paying your respects to Nike. The goddess of Victory is a valuable friend."

Luko, Tomas, and Uncle Demetrios head out to their patron's encampment, where they are staying while in Elis for the Olympics.

"Timon, wouldn't you have liked to see Uncle Demetrios run in the 85th Olympiad?" Luko asks Tomas. "He was a great runner and won many crowns."

"That was twenty years ago," says Demetrios with a chuckle. "Timon will soon break my record, I am sure."

"I'll never forget the first time you competed at Nemea, dear brother," says Luko, putting an arm across Tomas's shoulder. "You won the wild celery crown! I hope you will collect an olive crown at this Olympiad."

"And I hope you do, too," says Tomas.

The three have come over a ridge. Ahead, Tomas sees a large, decorated tent. Behind it are smaller tents and an enclosure for horses.

Inside the large tent, everyone lies on cushioned couches to eat. A girl, the first Tomas has seen anywhere, brings bread, olives, grilled fish, goat cheese, figs, and grapes. She is about his own age.

"Your patron went to inform the council that Luko will be his charioteer," says the girl. "He says you are to eat without him."

"Thank you, Daria," says Uncle Demetrios.

"Daria, are you coming to the Olympiad?" asks Tomas.

Daria tosses her head. "And dishonor myself by breaking the rule? No. We women go to honor Hera at the women's games—where *you* cannot go!"

"I am happy to see some rules are still followed," says Demetrios with a sigh. "Sparta did not honor the rules and is banned from the Olympiad."

"Sparta did more than just break the rules," says Luko. "Sparta declared war on Elis, the sacred home of Zeus."

After dinner, they go to a smaller tent with beds for each of them.

"Socrates says things are always changing," says Luko. "He says it is good to question. That way, you are sure whatever you do still comes from truth."

"I told you to stay away from his bad influence!" Demetrios is suddenly angry.

"The Oracle at Delphi says that Socrates is the wisest man there is," Luko answers calmly.

"The Oracle is known to speak in riddles," Demetrios answers.

After Demetrios blows out the oil lamp Tomas stares into the dark. *In our time everyone thinks Socrates is one of the greatest philosophers who ever lived. Why did Uncle Demetrios say those things?*

Tomas is too tired to think about it any more and soon he is sound asleep.

"Hurry, if you want to see anything." Demetrios shakes Tomas awake early the next morning. "People slept on the slopes by the stadium to get good places!"

When they arrive at the stadium, they find that the other boys and trainers have held places for them. A trumpet fanfare sounds.

"Here they come!" cries Milo.

The Hellenic Judges parade in, wearing purple robes. They sit on a row of stone seats—the only seats in the stadium. Tomas is happy to sit on the soft grass of the hillside.

Next, the chariots enter and take their places behind the starting gates. Trumpets give a signal, the gates are cranked open, and the chariots thunder off. By the first turn, some chariots have already crashed into each other or have lost wheels. Some horses have stumbled. But Luko drives so well that in the last lap, he and only one other chariot are left in the race.

Tomas and his friends cheer wildly. Luko finishes a close second.

"He has done well for one so young," Demetrios says proudly.

"May the Boeotian who owns the winning chariot step forward!" a voice booms.

A young man in a plain tunic pushes through from the back of the crowd. He bows to claim the crown.

"Stop! That man is an impostor!" calls out a councilman near the judge's stand. "I know him. He is a Spartan called Lichas! Because Sparta was banned from the games, he falsely called himself Boeotian to enter!"

The crowd begins to shout angrily. "This man is disqualified," proclaims the High Hellenic Judge. "He has dishonored the sacred Olympiad of Zeus. Take him away! The Athenian chariot wins!"

The angry shouts turn to cheers. Luko stands solemnly while his patron, the owner of the chariot, accepts the olive crown.

On the day of the Boy's 200-Meter Race, Tomas, Milo, and the others line up at a stone sill across one end of the long stadium. Tomas looks down at his bare toes wrapped over the starting stones. He remembers what Luko had told him in their tent the night before.

"Winning the chariot race because the other owner was disqualified is not a true win," Luko had said. "It is up to you now to bring honor to Athens. If Nike is your friend, you can't lose!"

If you are my friend, run with me, Nike! Tomas thinks. He tries to imagine Nike's wings on his feet.

The signal comes and he takes off. *Nike! Nike!* his mind says in time to his running feet. The crowd is a blur. He hears breathing as Milo passes him. Tomas digs down inside himself.

Nike! Nike! Nike! His feet hardly touch the ground as he runs faster than he's ever run before. With his heart pounding he passes Milo at the finish. He hears roaring and cheering. Suddenly, people are crowding around and patting his back. Demetrios grins and hugs him and Luko leaps around, yelling, "Praise to Nike! Honor for Athens!"

"I won!" Tomas shouts. Standing in front of the judges, he bows his head to receive the olive-leaf crown.

That night the patron gives a banquet in his tent. Daria and others girls dance and sing to the music of lyres, flutes, and bells. There is delicious food. Tomas, Luko, Uncle Demetrios, and the guests relax on the couches. Then the patron stands up. He is holding a wide, flat goblet in both hands.

"This kylix was my grandfather's. I use these goblets only for great occasions. Lift them to toast these brothers— the pride of Athens!"

"To Timon and Luko, the pride of Athens!" say the guests, raising their kylixes. As they drink, Tomas can see that a face is painted on the bottom of each goblet.

An oil lamp sputters. Smoke drifts up and he blinks several times.

"Tomas! You've been staring at that pottery for ages!" calls Lucy. "Come get in the picture!"

Tomas rubs his eyes. Emma and Kevin stand in front of the Acropolis display.

"Okay . . . ready?" says Lucy, as Tomas gets in place.

"Hey!" says Tomas as he feels a tug at his hair.

"Sorry," says Emma, "but I didn't think you'd want this hanging out of your hair in the picture."

Emma is holding an olive leaf! Tomas takes the leaf and smiles. *Thanks, Nike!* he thinks, as he slips it in his pocket. He looks at the camera.

"Okay, everyone . . . say 'NIKE!'" he says.

"NI . . . KE!" they all sing out. Lucy snaps the picture.

As the four cross the National Mall later, Tomas asks Kevin, "In those coins you were looking at, did any show Zeus on a throne with Nike standing in his hand?"

"I didn't see one exactly like that," Kevin says. "Why?"

"I was just curious." Tomas shrugs. "Come on, I'll race you to the bus!"

31

ABOUT GREECE IN 420 B.C.

In the fifth century B.C., the cities of Greece were organized as states, each with its own government and military. The city-state of Athens was ruled by Pericles, a great warrior and patron of the arts. He had the Parthenon built as a temple to honor Athena, the daughter of Zeus and the goddess of War. The Parthenon was built on the Acropolis, a flat-topped hill. When we think of Greece, we often think of the Parthenon, and tourists still go to see its ruins.

The first Olympiad was held in 776 B.C. in Olympia, a wooded valley in the city-state of Elis, as part of a religious festival. The only event was a 200-meter sprint. Instead of medals, athletes won olive crowns made from an olive tree behind the temple of Zeus. Athletes for the games were sponsored by rich and powerful men called patrons. Patrons paid all expenses, provided trainers, and often kept the athletes in their homes as part of their families.

The Olympics were held every four years, as they still are today. Soon after the first Olympiad, other events were added, such as chariot races and wrestling. The Olympiad lasted for five days.

In addition to the athletic events, there were religious ceremonies and a banquet at the end.

The city-states in ancient Greece often fought between themselves over boundaries or trade routes. At the time of a festival, a truce was declared so that people could travel to and from the games in safety. City-states would pick up their wars again when the truce ended.

In 420 B.C., Sparta would not obey the truce, and was banned from the Olympic games. Lichas, the Spartan in this story who tried to enter the 420 B.C. Olympiad disguised as a Boeotian, was a real person. He had trained his horses for so long that he could not stand it when his city-state's war on Elis caused Sparta to be banned.

Around 437 B.C., a sculptor named Pheidias was invited to create a statue of Zeus for the temple in Olympia. Pheidias had just finished the statue of Athena for the Parthenon in Athens. His Zeus was so amazing that it became one of the Seven Wonders of the Ancient World. The statue was destroyed by fire 800 years later. What we know of it comes from coins, drawings, and writings of people who saw it.

GLOSSARY

acropolis: A flat-topped hill.

chiton: A short tunic, usually made of linen. It was worn belted and might be plain or might have woven, embroidered, or painted borders. Women's chitons were worn to the ankle and men's were worn to the knee.

ebony wood: A smooth, fine grained, black wood.

kylix: A wide, shallow drinking cup with a stem and two handles, usually made of glazed terra-cotta pottery.